Arizona

BY ANN HEINRICHS

Content Adviser: Jennifer Lei Jenkins, Assistant Professor of Humanities, University of Arizona, Tucson, Arizona

Reading Adviser: Dr. Linda D. Labbo, Department of Reading Education, College of Education, The University of Georgia

COMPASS POINT BOOKS  MINNEAPOLIS, MINNESOTA

Compass Point Books
3109 West 50th Street, #115
Minneapolis, MN 55410

Visit Compass Point Books on the Internet at *www.compasspointbooks.com*
or e-mail your request to *custserv@compasspointbooks.com*

On the cover: Mission San Xavier del Bac, just outside Tucson, on the San Xavier Reservation

Photographs ©: Buddy Mays/Travel Stock Photography, cover, 1; Thomas Kitchin/Tom Stack &
Associates, 3, 12; Corbis, 5, 42; Robert Fried/Tom Stack & Associates, 6, 48 (top); Martin G.
Miller/Visuals Unlimited, 7, 47; Milton Rand/Tom Stack & Associates, 8, 45; Susan A. Levine
Photographic Art/Lbd Associates, 9; Doug Sokell/Visuals Unlimited, 10, 44 (top); Tom Bean/Corbis, 13;
Hulton/Archive by Getty Images, 14, 16 (top), 18, 46; James P. Rowan, 15, 40; Bettmann/Corbis, 16
(bottom); Brian Parker/Tom Stack & Associates, 17; Unicorn Stock Photos/Andre Jenny, 20, 22; John Elk
III, 23, 26, 27, 29, 36 (bottom), 41; Collection, The Supreme Court Historical Society/Richard Strauss,
Smithsonian Institution, 24; Unicorn Stock Photos/Phyllis Kedl, 25; Photo Network/Mark Newman, 28,
43; Charles Rushing/Visuals Unlimited, 30; Peter Harholt/Corbis, 31; Walt Anderson/Visuals Unlimited,
32; Jan Butchofsky-Hauser/Corbis, 33; Unicorn Stock Photos/Richard Gilbert, 34; Galen Rowell/Corbis,
35; Buddy Mays/Corbis, 36 (top); Jeff Greenberg/Visuals Unlimited, 38; Unicorn Stock Photos/H.
Schmeiser, 39; Robesus, Inc., 43 (state flag); One Mile Up, Inc., 43 (state seal); Joe McDonald/Visuals
Unlimited, 44 (middle); PhotoDisc, 44 (bottom).

Editors: E. Russell Primm, Emily J. Dolbear, and Patricia Stockland
Photo Researcher: Marcie C. Spence
Photo Selector: Linda S. Koutris
Designer: The Design Lab
Cartographer: XNR Productions, Inc.

Library of Congress Cataloging-in-Publication Data
Heinrichs, Ann.
 Arizona / by Ann Heinrichs.
   p. cm.— (This land is your land)
Includes bibliographical references (p.) and index.
Contents: Welcome to Arizona!—Canyons, deserts, and plateaus—A trip through time—Government by
the people—Arizonans at work—Getting to know Arizonans—Let's explore Arizona!
 ISBN 0-7565-0333-7
1. Arizona—Juvenile literature. [1. Arizona.] I. Title. II. Series.
 F811.3 .H454 2003
 979.1—dc21   2002012862

Table of Contents

NOTE: In this book, words that are defined in the glossary are in **bold** the first time they appear in the text.

"And what a world of grandeur is spread before us!" John Wesley Powell wrote these words in 1869. He was exploring the Colorado River through Arizona's Grand Canyon. Powell gazed in awe at the brightly colored, steep-walled canyon. He called it "the most sublime spectacle of nature."

Arizona's nickname is the Grand Canyon State. More than 4 million people visit this spectacular canyon every year. Arizona also has vast stretches of desert. Brilliant red rock formations rise up from the desert floor.

Arizona's history is as colorful as its land. Many ruins remain from prehistoric times. Ancient people built homes in the steep cliff sides. They dug **canals** to water their desert crops. Later, miners and gunfighters came to make their fortunes.

Today, Arizona is a leader in making electronics and spacecraft. Its farms produce tons of cotton, vegetables, and fruits. Arizona is also one of America's fastest-growing states. Thousands of new residents move in every year. They enjoy its natural beauty and warm climate. Now explore Arizona, and you'll enjoy it, too!

▲ Arizona is known as the Grand Canyon State.

Canyons, Deserts, and Plateaus

Arizona is one of the southwestern states, and it's big!
Only five states are larger. Arizona also has five neighbors.
North of Arizona is Utah. New Mexico lies to the east.
Nevada and California are on the west. To the south is the
country of Mexico.

▲ **The Colorado River cuts into the Grand Canyon.**

▲ Lake Mead, the largest human-made lake in the United States

The Colorado River flows across northeastern Arizona. Along the way, it cuts deep into solid rock. Among its many canyons is the Grand Canyon. It took millions of years to create this deep gorge. The Colorado River also forms most of Arizona's western border.

Many dams have been built on Arizona's rivers and provide **irrigation** for crops. Theodore Roosevelt Lake was built on the Salt River in 1911. Lakes Powell, Mead, and Havasu

▲ **The Camel Butte rock formation in Monument Valley**

lie along the Colorado River. Arizona shares these three lakes with neighboring states. Lake Mead is the largest human-made lake in the United States.

Northern Arizona is part of what is called the Colorado **Plateau.** The northeastern part of the state has many amazing natural sights. One is Monument Valley. Its strange rock formations rise up from the ground like monuments to Earth's earlier days. Black **Mesa** is a group of high, flat-topped mountains. The Painted Desert looks like it has been painted many

▲ **Mogollon Rim**

colors. Within this desert is the **Petrified** Forest. Giant logs lie on the ground. They have turned to stone over millions of years.

The Colorado Plateau's southern end is the Mogollon Rim. It's a steep wall of rock. South of the rim are many forest-covered mountain ranges.

The Basin and Range region includes southern and western Arizona. That area is often called the Sonoran Desert.

Arizona's largest cities are in this region. They include Tucson, Mesa, and Phoenix, the state capital. Some mountains run through this area, but in between them are broad, flat deserts.

Organ-pipe, prickly pear, and cholla cactus grow in the deserts. The giant saguaro is the biggest cactus of them all. It has long "arms" that extend upward. Cactus wrens build

▲ Many different types of cacti grow in the Sonoran Desert.

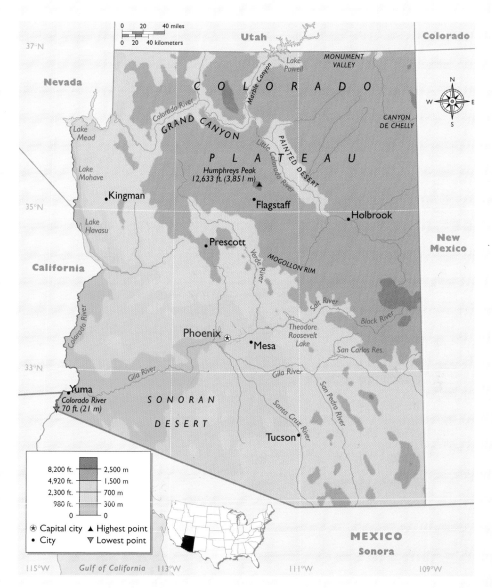

▲ **A topographic map of Arizona**

nests in holes in the saguaros. **Javelinas,** mule deer, and

rattlesnakes are some other desert creatures. Coyotes can

be heard howling in the night.

Forests grow on Arizona's mountains and plateaus. There you'll find deer, bobcats, cougars, and bears. Bighorn sheep scramble across the mountainsides.

Animals aren't the only ones enjoying Arizona. Even in the 1800s, people traveled to Arizona for their health. The dry desert air is good for many health problems. Arizona's mountains and plateaus are cool all year round. Temperatures are warmest in the southwest. Summers in the desert can be quite hot. When winter comes, however, the desert is warm.

▲ Cougars, also known as mountain lions, roam Arizona's forests.

That's when people from cold northern states pour in. Not everyone heads for the deserts, though. People who ski love Arizona's snowy mountains.

▲ Skiers enjoy the snow at Coconino National Forest in Flagstaff.

A Trip Through Time

People lived in Arizona more than two thousand years ago.
The ancient Pueblo people occupied the northern plateaus.
They built their pueblos, or towns, in the cliffs. Today's Hopi
Indians are their descendants. The Hohokam lived in the
southern deserts. They dug irrigation canals from the rivers.
The Hohokam are the ancestors of today's Pima and Tohono
O'odham people. Eastern Arizona was home to the Mogollon.
They hunted wild animals and gathered nuts and berries.
Later the Navajo, Apache, and other groups moved in.

▲ A Hopi town built on a cliff

Spanish explorers were the first Europeans in Arizona. Francisco Vásquez de Coronado claimed Arizona for Spain in 1540. Father Eusebio Kino worked among the Indians in the late 1600s. He taught farming methods and set up missions.

In 1752, Spaniards built their first permanent settlement at Tubac. They opened a fort at Tucson in 1776. Mexico gained independence from Spain in 1821. Then Arizona belonged to Mexico. The United States won most of Arizona in 1848 after a war with Mexico. The Gadsden Purchase in 1853 added southern Arizona to the United States.

Arizona Territory was created in 1863. Indians fought to hold on to their land. One

▲ **A statue of Father Eusebio Kino located in Phoenix**

▲ Apache leader Geronimo

▲ A photograph of Wyatt Earp five years after the shootout at the OK Corral

by one, though, they were defeated. Geronimo and his Chiricahua Apaches were the last to go, in 1886. Meanwhile, miners were discovering rich mineral deposits. They found gold in the 1850s and silver in the 1870s. By the 1880s, copper was Arizona's top mineral.

"Boomtowns" grew up around each new mine site. They were rowdy towns full of gamblers, gunfighters, and outlaws. Wyatt Earp was the deputy U.S. marshal in Tombstone, one rowdy boomtown. In 1881, he faced a band of outlaws. They had a famous shootout at the OK Corral.

Meanwhile, other settlers were farming. They raised cotton, vegetables, cattle, and sheep. People discovered the old Hohokam irrigation canals and rebuilt them. Once again, crops thrived in the Salt River Valley. The city of Phoenix grew up there.

Arizona became the forty-eighth state in 1912. By that time, tourism was becoming a growing business. As Arizona grew, so did the need for water. Many dams were built on southwestern rivers. They provided irrigation and water-powered electricity.

▲ Hoover Dam is on the Colorado River in Nevada. It created Lake Mead, which Arizona and Nevada share.

▲ Navajo Indians working on a railroad in Yuma in 1942 as part of the war effort

Arizonans helped out during World War II (1939–1945). They sent cotton, copper, and beef as war supplies. Many soldiers and pilots trained in Arizona, too. The Navajo Codetalkers played a very important role during the war. The complex Navajo language was used as a code that the enemies were never able to break. The careful work of the Codetalkers helped win the war and save many lives.

Air-conditioning arrived in the 1950s. This made Arizona even more attractive to outsiders. Sun City opened in 1960. It was the first of many communities for retired people. Many new factories sprang up in the 1970s. Again, all this growth called for more water. The Central Arizona Project opened in 1985. It brought water from the Colorado River to central Arizona.

Today, Arizona is more popular than ever. People visit for its climate, scenery, and historic sites. Many visitors decide to stay permanently.

Government by the People

Arizona has changed its capital many times. Fort Whipple was Arizona Territory's first capital. It changed to Prescott, then Tucson, then Prescott again. Phoenix has been the capital since 1889.

Arizona's state government works just like the U.S.

▲ **The state capitol in Phoenix**

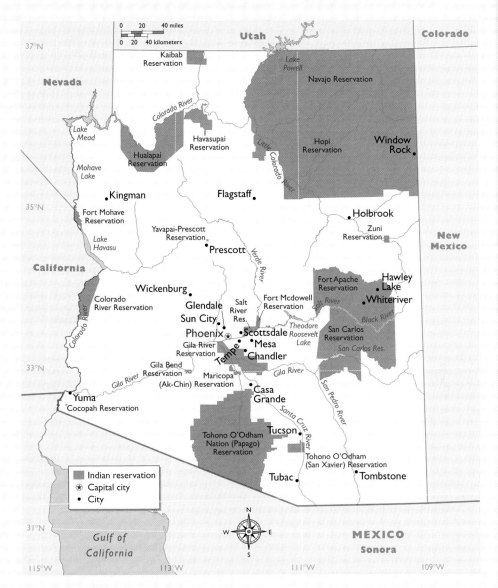

▲ A geopolitical map of Arizona

government. It's divided into three branches—executive,

legislative, and judicial. The three branches make for a

good balance of power.

▲ A meeting of the house of representatives in the state capitol

The executive branch carries out the state's laws. The governor is the head of the executive branch. Arizonans vote for a governor every four years. The governor can serve only two terms in a row. Voters also elect other high-ranking executive officers.

The legislative branch makes the state laws. Voters elect their lawmakers to serve in Arizona's legislature. The legislature has two houses, or parts. One is the thirty-member senate. The other is the sixty-member house of representatives. All lawmakers serve two-year terms. They are limited to four terms in a row. The lawmakers meet in the state capitol in Phoenix.

The judicial branch is made up of judges. They are experts in the law. They decide whether someone has broken a law. Arizona's highest court is the state supreme court. It has five judges.

Arizona is divided into fifteen counties. Voters in each county elect county officers. A community with 1,500 people can become an official city or town. Most

▲ Judges hear a variety of cases in this Pima County courthouse in Tucson.

▲ Arizonans William Rehnquist (front row, center) and Sandra Day O'Connor (front row, second from right) have played important roles in the U.S. Supreme Court.

cities and towns are governed by an elected council. One council member becomes the mayor, or manager. Cities may choose to have home rule. Then they can choose a different form of government.

Many Arizonans have been in the national spotlight. Arizona senator Barry Goldwater ran for president in 1964. Carl Hayden served in the U.S. Congress for fifty-seven years. Sandra Day O'Connor became a U.S. Supreme Court justice in 1981. She was the court's first female justice. Arizonan William Rehnquist joined the Supreme Court in 1972. He became its chief justice in 1986.

The dome and roof on Arizona's state capitol are nice and shiny. Why? Because they're made of copper. How much copper? Fifteen tons (13,608 kilograms)! That's enough to make millions of pennies.

Arizona leads the nation in mining copper. Arizona's mines still produce gold and silver, too. Other mining products are coal, sand, gravel, and crushed stone.

▲ **A copper mine in Bisbee**

▲ In addition to manufacturing airplanes and helicopters, Arizonans also make missiles.

Arizona's top factory goods are electronics equipment. That includes computer chips and other computer parts. Next in value are air and space vehicles. Arizona factories make airplanes, helicopters, missiles, and other spacecraft. Many electronics and aircraft plants are near Phoenix and Tucson. Other factory goods include foods, metals, and machines.

More than half of Arizona's land area is grazing land. Cattle and calves bring in the most farm income. Milk and other dairy products are next in value. Many Navajo people raise sheep for wool. Some also raise Angora goats for their silky mohair wool.

Arizona's warm climate is great for farmers. They can grow many vegetables in the winter. Then they sell the

▲ **Sheep on a Navajo reservation**

▲ Cotton is a major
Arizona crop.

vegetables to colder states. After California, Arizona is the top producer of a whole list of crops. They include lettuce, cauliflower, broccoli, cantaloupes, and honeydews. Some farmers raise citrus fruits such as lemons, tangerines, and oranges. Arizona ranks third in tangerines and fourth in oranges, grapefruit, and durum wheat. Arizona is also a leading cotton producer and ranks third in pima cotton.

However, most workers in Arizona sell services instead of products. Service workers include teachers, engineers, and health care workers. Many work at Arizona's military bases. Some sell homes to new residents. Others work in the tourist trade. They all use their skills to help others.

Getting to Know Arizonans

Arizona is growing fast! In 2000, there were 5,130,632 people in Arizona. That's almost seven times the 1950 count! During the 1990s, only Nevada grew faster than Arizona.

Almost nine of every ten Arizonans live in city areas. Phoenix is the largest city, followed by Tucson. The next-

▲ **Fifth Avenue Fountain in Scottsdale, one of Arizona's largest cities**

largest cities are all clustered near Phoenix. They include Mesa, Glendale, Scottsdale, Chandler, and Tempe. This region is often called the Valley of the Sun—or just the Valley.

One of every four Arizonans is Hispanic. They belong to Mexican and other Spanish-speaking cultures. Mexican foods are popular in Arizona. So are Mexican festivals. Cinco de Mayo (May 5) and Mexican Independence Day (September 16) are big events. They're colorful celebrations with music, dancing, and food.

One of every twenty Arizonans is Native American. Most live on one of the twenty **reservations.** Arizona is home to seventeen different Native American tribes, including Navajo, Hopi, Apache, Pima, Tohono O'odham, and

▲ A woman in traditional Mexican dress during a Cinco de Mayo celebration in Mesa

Yuma. The Tohono O'odham are also called the Papago. The largest group by far is the Navajo. Their reservation is the biggest in the nation.

Native American crafts include pottery, blankets, rugs, and baskets. Each tribe has its own special patterns. The Navajo make silver and turquoise jewelry. The Hopi make kachinas, or carved wooden spirit figures. The Hopi are also famous for their pottery, which continues a tradition begun by their ancestors.

Many groups hold pow-wows, dances, and other ceremonies. They include the Navajo Nation Fair in Window Rock and the Tohono O'odham festival in Casa Grande. The White Mountain Apache hold a fair and rodeo in Whiteriver.

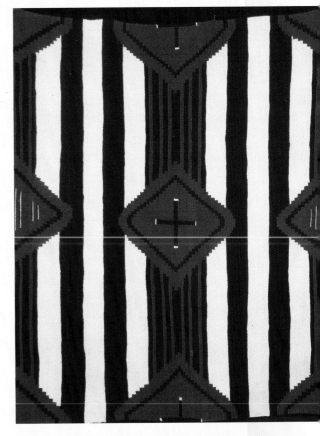

▲ This Navajo blanket is an example of the many Native American crafts you might find in Arizona.

▲ **Prescott is well known for its rodeos.**

Before Easter, the Yaqui present a Passion play in Tucson. It's a blend of tribal and Christian customs.

Arizona's cowboy culture comes out in many ways. One is "cowboy food" such as chili and barbecued beef. Cowboys also show off their skills in rodeos. Prescott held its first rodeo in 1888. Now it holds the "World's Oldest Rodeo" every July. La Fiesta de los Vaqueros is a rodeo held in Tucson.

Scottsdale holds the Thunderbird Balloon Classic for hot air balloon fans. Wickenburg celebrates Gold Rush Days. New Year's is Fiesta Bowl time. There's a parade in Phoenix and a college football game in Tempe.

▲ **Hot air balloons at the Thunderbird Balloon Classic in Scottsdale**

▲ The America West Arena in Phoenix is where the Suns and the Mercury play.

Phoenix is a hot spot for sports. It's home to the Arizona Cardinals football team and the Phoenix Suns and Phoenix Mercury basketball teams. The Phoenix Coyotes play hockey. Phoenix got the Arizona Diamondbacks baseball team in 1998. The Diamondbacks won the 2001 World Series.

Let's Explore Arizona!

Gaze down into the Grand Canyon and you feel small. You are seeing the effects of millions of years of history. From where you stand, it's about a mile (1.6 km) to the bottom! For a closer look, ride a mule down into the canyon. Some people say mules are stubborn. Really, they're just careful. They plod safely down the steep canyon walls. There are many other scenic canyons along the river. They include Havasu Canyon, Marble Canyon, and Glen Canyon.

You could spend weeks exploring northeastern Arizona. The Navajo Indian reservation covers most of this area. It

▲ **Falls in Havasu Canyon**

▲ A giant stone log in the Petrified Forest

▲ Rock formations reflect in Oak Creek in Sedona.

completely surrounds the Hopi reservation. The Hopi villages are perched high on three mesas. One village is Oraibi. People have lived there since about 1100.

In Monument Valley, tall rocks tower above the desert floor. Canyon de Chelly has many ancient Pueblo Indian cliff dwellings. Giant logs—now stone—are scattered around the Petrified Forest. Saguaro National Park protects thousands of giant saguaro cacti.

Near Flagstaff is Sunset Crater. A volcano erupted here almost a thousand years ago. Nearby are Wupatki and Walnut Canyon national monuments. Both sites have hundreds of ancient Sinagua Indian dwellings. Down in Oak Creek Canyon is Sed-

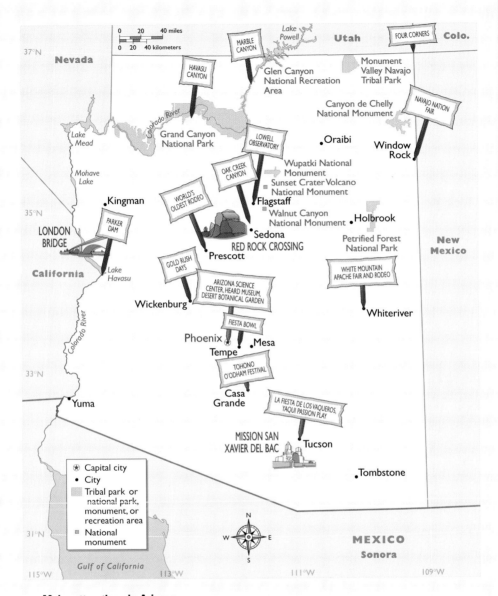

▲ **Major attractions in Arizona**

ona. Beautiful red rock formations rise in every direction.

You may think you've seen Red Rock Crossing before. Many

Western movies have been filmed in this area.

Did you ever sing the tune "London Bridge is Falling Down"? London Bridge is standing up just fine now. It stretches over Lake Havasu in western Arizona. Piece by piece, the bridge was taken apart in London, England. Then workers put it back together here. Parker Dam created Lake Havasu along the Colorado River. Farther north is Lake Mead.

▲ **London Bridge in western Arizona**

Tall palm trees line the streets of Phoenix, Arizona's capital. The Arizona Science Center includes a planetarium and a giant five-story theater. You'll explore Indian history and culture in the Heard Museum. Hundreds of desert plants thrive in the Desert Botanical Garden. South of Phoenix is Casa Grande. The Hohokam Indians built its tall tower hundreds of years ago.

Tucson lies in a desert valley surrounded by mountains. Look out across the desert, and you see giant saguaro cactus plants. Near Tucson is Mission San Xavier

▲ A selection of Arizona plants in the Desert Botanical Garden

▲ **White Dove of the Desert Church at Mission San Xavier del Bac**

del Bac, on the San Xavier Reservation in the Tohono O'odham Nation. Its gleaming white church is called the White Dove of the Desert.

Arizona has many more ancient villages and stunning natural sites. Just one visit is not enough to explore it all. You'll want to come back for more!

Important Dates

1064   Sunset Crater erupts.

1540   Francisco Vásquez de Coronado leads an expedition into Arizona and claims it for Spain.

1680   Hopi Indians take part in the Pueblo Revolt.

1691   Father Eusebio Kino establishes missions at Guevavi, Tumacacori, and San Xavier del Bac. He brings cattle, wheat, and pomegranates, as well as Christianity, to the region.

1821   Arizona becomes part of Mexico.

1848   After the Mexican War (1846–1848), most of Arizona passes to the United States.

1853   In the Gadsden Purchase, the United States gains more Arizona land.

1863   Arizona Territory is created.

1869   John Wesley Powell explores the Grand Canyon.

1886   University of Arizona is founded.

1911   Theodore Roosevelt Dam opens on the Salt River.

1912   Arizona becomes the forty-eighth U.S. state on February 14.

1919   Grand Canyon National Park is established.

1966   *Miranda* v. *Arizona* ensures that people under arrest must be "read their rights."

1974   Raul Castro is elected Arizona's first Hispanic governor.

1981   Sandra Day O'Connor of Arizona is the first woman on the U.S. Supreme Court.

1985   The Central Arizona Project is completed.

2001   The Arizona Diamondbacks win the World Series.

Glossary

canals—human-made waterways

irrigation—a way of bringing water to fields through canals or ditches

javelinas—a type of wild pig

mesa—a flat-topped mountain

petrified—made into stone over time by taking in water and dissolved minerals

plateau—high, flat land

reservations—large areas of land set aside for Native Americans

Did You Know?

★ Astronomers at Lowell Observatory in Flagstaff discovered the planet Pluto in 1930.

★ Arizona, New Mexico, Colorado, and Utah meet at four equal angles. This point is called Four Corners.

★ Arizona is home to eleven species of rattlesnake.

★ Gunsight, Ruby, and Gillett are some of Arizona's ghost towns.

★ Among all the states, Arizona has the largest percentage of its land set aside for Native American use.

★ Phoenix was named after a mythical bird. This bird died in flames and then rose again from the ashes.

★ The Phoenix area had once been a thriving Hohokam settlement. Then the city of Phoenix rose up over the Hohokam ruins.

★ The Petrified Forest is the world's largest collection of petrified wood.

★ The Hopi village of Oraibi is the nation's oldest settlement where people have lived continuously. People have lived at Oraibi since at least 1100.

State capital: Phoenix

State motto: *Ditat Deus* (Latin for "God Enriches")

State nickname: Grand Canyon State

Statehood: February 14, 1912; forty-eighth state

Land area: 113,642 square miles (376,990 sq km); **rank:** sixth

Highest point: Humphreys Peak, 12,633 feet (3,851 m) above sea level

Lowest point: Along the Colorado River in Yuma County, 70 feet (21 m) above sea level

Highest recorded temperature: 128°F (53°C) at Lake Havasu City on June 29, 1994

Lowest recorded temperature: −40°F (−40°C) at Hawley Lake on January 7, 1971

Average January temperature: 41°F (5°C)

Average July temperature: 80°F (27°C)

Population in 2000: 5,130,632; **rank:** twentieth

Largest cities in 2000: Phoenix (1,321,045), Tucson (486,699), Mesa (396,375), Glendale (218,812)

Factory products: Computer parts, transportation equipment, chemicals

Farm products: Beef cattle, cotton, lettuce

Mining products: Copper, gold, silver

State flag: In the middle of Arizona's state flag is a star. It's the color of copper, Arizona's leading mineral. Thirteen red and yellow rays stream out from the star. Some people say they represent the thirteen original colonies and others say they represent the thirteen original counties of Arizona. They also represent the setting sun. Red and yellow were the colors of the Spanish flag Coronado carried into Arizona in the 1500s. The bottom half of the flag's background is the blue of the American flag.

State seal: The state seal shows a shield containing symbols for Arizona's farming, cattle-raising, and mining industries. A dam stands for the importance of water in Arizona. In the background, the sun rises over mountains. This stands for Arizona's climate. At the top of the shield is the state motto. At the bottom of the seal is "1912," the date of statehood.

State abbreviations: Ariz. (traditional); AZ (postal)

State Symbols

State bird: Cactus wren

State flower: Saguaro blossom

State tree: Palo Verde

State mammal: Ringtail

State fish: Apache trout

State reptile: Arizona ridgenose rattlesnake

State amphibian: Arizona tree frog

State gemstone: Turquoise

State fossil: Petrified wood

State neckwear: Bola tie

State colors: Blue and gold

Making Arizona Chicken Chili

Chili is a favorite Arizona dish—and this one uses chicken.

Makes five servings.

INGREDIENTS:

1 pound chicken breast meat

1 tablespoon vegetable oil

2 tablespoons Southwestern-
   style spice blend

1 can diced tomatoes

1 can corn

1 can kidney beans

Shredded cheese

DIRECTIONS:

Make sure an adult helps with the cutting and the hot stove. Cut chicken into 1-inch cubes. Heat oil in a skillet. Add chicken and cook 5 to 6 minutes. Stir in the remaining ingredients except for the cheese. Cook until it begins to bubble. Lower the heat and simmer 10 minutes. Serve with cheese sprinkled on top.

"Arizona March Song"

Words by Margaret Rowe Clifford, music by Maurice Blumenthal

Come to this land of sunshine
To this land where life is young.
Where the wide, wide world is waiting,
The songs that will now be sung.
Where the golden sun is flaming
Into warm, white, shining day,
And the sons of men are blazing
Their priceless right of way.

Come stand beside the rivers
Within our valleys broad.
Stand here with heads uncovered,
In the presence of our God!
While all around, about us
The brave, unconquered band,
As guardians and landmarks
The giant mountains stand.

Not alone for gold and silver
Is Arizona great.
But with graves of heroes sleeping,
All the land is consecrate!
O, come and live beside us
However far ye roam
Come and help us build up temples
And name those temples "home."

Chorus:
Sing the song that's in your hearts
Sing of the great Southwest,
Thank God, for Arizona
In splendid sunshine dressed.
For thy beauty and thy grandeur,
For thy regal robes so sheen
We hail thee Arizona
Our Goddess and our queen.

Bruce Babbitt (1938–) was secretary of the interior under President Bill Clinton (1993–2001) and Arizona's governor from 1978 to 1987.

Frank Borman (1928–) was one of the original seven *Mercury* astronauts.

Cesar Chavez (1927–1993) was a labor leader who worked for the rights of farm-workers, especially Mexican migrant work-ers. He organized the United Farm Workers union and gained workers' rights through boycotts and strikes.

Wyatt Earp (1848–1929) was the deputy marshal in Tombstone at the time of the shootout at the OK Corral.

Geronimo (1829–1909) was a Chiricahua Apache chief who led his people in fighting the U.S. government. Geronimo (pictured above left) escaped many captures but final-ly surrendered in 1886.

Barry Goldwater (1909–1998) was chair-man of the Armed Services and Intelligence committees while serving in the U.S. Senate. He ran for president in 1964 but lost to Lyndon B. Johnson.

Carl Hayden (1877–1972) represented Arizona in the U.S. Congress for fifty-seven years (1912–1969). Thanks to his efforts, Congress passed the Central Arizona Project.

Ira Hamilton Hayes (1923–1955) was a Pima Marine who helped to raise the American flag after the battle at Iwo Jima, Japan, during World War II.

Father Eusebio Kino (1645–1711) was a Jesuit missionary. He established twenty-seven missions and introduced crops and cattle raising to the Indians. Kino is called the "Padre on Horseback." He was born in Italy.

John McCain (1936–) is a U.S. senator from Arizona. He was born in the Panama Canal Zone.

Sandra Day O'Connor (1930–) is the first woman associate justice of the U.S. Supreme Court. She was appointed in 1981. She was born in Texas.

Charles Poston (1825–1902) is called the "Father of Arizona." He was a miner and in 1864 became Arizona Territory's first repre-sentative in the U.S. Congress.

John Wesley Powell (1834–1902) was a geologist, or scientist who studies Earth's history through its rocks. He explored the Green and Colorado Rivers, including the Grand Canyon.

William Rehnquist (1924–) became an associate justice of the U.S. Supreme Court in 1972 and chief justice in 1986. He was born in Wisconsin.

Linda Ronstadt (1946–) is a singer. She has recorded rock, jazz, country, and Latin songs and has won seven Grammy awards. Her ancestors were Mexican pioneers in Territorial Tucson.

Stewart Udall (1920–) served as U.S. secretary of the interior from 1961 to 1969.

Want to Know More?

At the Library

Dawavendewa, Gerald. *The Butterfly Dance.* New York: Abbeville Press, 2001.

Filbin, Dan. *Arizona.* Minneapolis: Lerner, 2002.

Minor, Wendell. *Grand Canyon: Exploring a Natural Wonder.* New York: Scholastic Trade, 1998.

Sekaquaptewa, Eugene, Emory Sekaquaptewa, and Barbara Pepper, editors. *Coyote and the Winnowing Birds: A Traditional Hopi Tale.* Santa Fe, N.M.: Clear Light Publishers, 1994.

Standard, Carole K. *Arizona.* Danbury, Conn.: Children's Press, 2002.

Thompson, Kathleen. *Arizona.* Austin, Tex.: Raintree/Steck-Vaughn, 1996.

On the Web

Arizona @ Your Service

http://www.az.gov

To learn about Arizona's history, culture, government, and economy

Arizona Tourism

http://www.arizonatourism.com/

To find out about Arizona's events, activities, and sights

Through the Mail

Arizona Office of Tourism

2702 N. 3rd Street, Suite 4015
Phoenix, AZ 85004
For information on travel and interesting sights in Arizona

Arizona Department of Commerce

3800 N. Central Avenue, Suite 1500
Phoenix, AZ 85012
For information on Arizona's economy

On the Road

Arizona State Capitol Complex

1700 West Washington
Phoenix, AZ 85007
602/542-4675
To visit Arizona's state capitol, museum, and other sites

Index

About the Author

Ann Heinrichs grew up in Fort Smith, Arkansas, and lives in Chicago. She is the author of more than one hundred books for children and young adults on Asian, African, and U.S. history and culture. Ann has also written numerous newspaper, magazine, and encyclopedia articles. She is an award-winning martial artist, specializing in t'ai chi empty-hand and sword forms.

Ann has traveled widely throughout the United States, Africa, Asia, and the Middle East. In exploring each state for this series, she rediscovered the people, history, and resources that make this a great land, as well as the concerns we share with people around the world.